ON THE DEVELOPMEN MEMORY AND IDENT

(Vol. 2, 1967 Heinz We Lecture Series)

by Jean Piaget

This is the second lecture given at Clark University in honor of the late Heinz Werner, world-famous developmental psychologist. In these two lectures, Professor Piaget raises fundamental questions concerning the nature of memory in the developing child and his response to invariance. In the first, "Memory and Operations", he examines the way in which memory schemata are transformed during the course of the formation of "concrete operations" in early childhood. In the second, "Identity and Conservation", he outlines a developmental sequence of identity responses, starting with simple recognition of persons in infancy and leading up to conservation as an understanding of the invariance of certain quantitative properties or attributes as an object is subjected to particular transformations.

Jean Piaget, Professor of Psychology and Director of the Pedagogical Sciences at the University of Geneva, is world renowned for his contributions to the development of perceptual and intellectual processes, to the theory and practice of education, to the history and theory of knowledge, and to the field of logic. The author of more than 30 major books and innumerable articles, Professor Piaget continues to be one of the seminal minds of the twentieth century.

ON THE DEVELOPMENT OF MEMORY AND IDENTITY

Drawing by Leonard Baskin

On the Development of Memory and Identity

by Jean Piaget

Translated by Eleanor Duckworth

CLARK UNIVERSITY PRESS

with BARRE PUBLISHERS

1968

Library of Congress Card Catalog Number 68-17071
Composed and printed by The Barre Publishing Company
Barre, Massachusetts

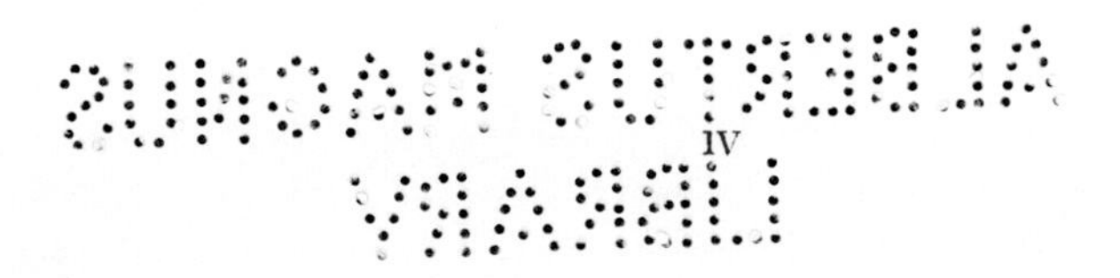

THE HEINZ WERNER LECTURES

THE HEINZ WERNER LECTURE SERIES

The Lecture Series, of which this volume is the second, is designed to provide a forum for outstanding scholars who are known for their contributions to the developmental analysis of biological, psychological and/ or socio-cultural phenomena. This Series is sponsored by the Heinz Werner Institute of Developmental Psychology.

Heinz Werner (1890-1964) was one of the leading psychologists of the past half-century. Deeply impressed by processes of organic formation and ordered change in various domains of the life sciences, he sought to apply developmental conceptualization and developmental analysis to all aspects of existence in which mentality is manifested. Convinced that developmental psychology is not merely a subject-matter but is, rather, a manner of conceptualizing all psychological phenomena, Werner sought to encompass animal behavior, ontogenesis, pathological phenomena, products of collective activity, and behavior evoked in experimental situations, within a comprehensive system — a general psychology, grounded in the fundamental concept of development. In accord with Werner's philosophy, the Heinz Werner Institute of Developmental Psychology is devoted to the application of developmental analysis to all psycho-biological and psycho-cultural phenomena. It seeks to fulfill Werner's vision by promoting research and teaching at graduate and post-graduate levels which will serve to integrate the various life sciences without collapsing their distinctiveness in method and subject-matter.

Bernard Kaplan
Seymour Wapner
Joachim F. Wohlwill

CONTENTS

MEMORY AND OPERATIONS OF INTELLIGENCE[1]

I SHOULD like first of all to express my thanks to Dr. Wapner for having invited me to give the Heinz Werner Memorial Lectures this year, thus permitting me to express the great admiration which I bear for Heinz Werner, the most comprehensive and most profound representative of developmental psychology in the United States in recent years. I have chosen to speak first about relations between memory and intelligence, because it is such an apt developmental problem, that is, one of those problems which cannot be resolved with any thoroughness unless we adopt the point of view of the formative mechanisms throughout childhood.

Changes in the code

It is customary to represent memory as a system of coding and decoding, which naturally assumes the intervention of a *code*. But, curiously enough, this code itself has been studied very little, as if it were taken for granted that the code stays the same throughout development. This assumption is not always made explicitly, but implicitly it is widespread, and it even seems obvious if the representative aspects of thought, that is, mental imagery (in the form of memory-images) and language, are considered as "copies" of an internal or external reality.

On the other hand, if one accepts our results concerning the operational development of thought, and if we thus admit the existence of a progressive structuring of reality by means of operations gradually constructed one after another or on the basis of one another, then the most likely hypothesis is that the memory code itself depends on the subject's operations, and that therefore this code is modified during development, and depends at any given moment on the subject's operational level.

But how can such an hypothesis be justified? With B. Inhelder, we have used a simple approach in a series of investigations soon to be published, namely, to study memory after different intervals of retention: for example, immediate memory (after one hour), a week later, and finally after several months (usually six months). If during the interval, the code remains the same, then we would expect the memory to stay unchanged, or else to deteriorate in quantity or quality, but it would seem impossible for memory to improve during an interval of several months. If, on the other hand, the memory code depends on the subject's operational level, and improves with the progress of the operations, then we could expect, in certain simple cases, an improvement in memory, in the richness of its content and above all in its structure. In the experiments we conducted, the encoding has in no way been modified (the model is never presented again, neither during the interval, nor at the time of the evocation of the memory); so that if the decoding is better some months later, it must have taken on new significance, due to the progress in the subject's operational schemata. It would seem that there is only one possible interpretation of such improvement, namely, that the code itself has changed and improved in the meantime.

(A) Let us look first at a small experiment from this perspective. The children are shown an ordered configuration, that is, 10 sticks, varying in size from about 9 to 15 centimeters, ordered from the biggest to the smallest. (The configuration is ready-made; the children are not required to construct it.) The children are asked to have a good look, so that they will be able to draw it later. A week later, without showing them the configuration again, they are asked to draw or to describe verbally (there were different experimental groups with different techniques) what we had shown them before. Six months later, without seeing the configuration, they were asked to do the same thing.

The first interesting result of this experiment concerns what we find after one week. We find that what the subject retains is not the perceptual model as such, but the way in which he assimilated it to his operational schemata, in terms of the operational level of each individual subject. The youngest (3-4 years) remember a form which we call *a*, which consists of a certain number of sticks lined up, but all the same length IIIII. Slightly older, (4-5 years) remember the model in a form which we shall call *b*, in which there are big sticks and small sticks, but only two sizes; they are presented either as repeated couples IıIıIı or as a dichotomous series: IIIııı. A slightly more advanced level presents triplets Iıılıı or IIIIIIııı; we shall call this form *c*. Five-to six year- olds generally attain form *d*, which is a small series of four or five elements. Finally, around 6 or 7 years of age, we find the form we shall call *e*, which is a series like the original one, with about 10 elements.

Now after six months all the subjects from 3 to 8 years claimed that they remembered very well what we had shown them. But interestingly enough, they generally did not give the same drawing or description. There was not one instance of deterioration in the memory in this experiment (although there were such instances in other experiments, for reasons which we shall see later); on the contrary 74% of the subjects had a *better* recollection now than they had after one week. The progress did not take the form of big leaps: we rarely saw a transition from *a*, or *b* to *e*. Usually we found an improvement from one level to the next: from equalities (*a*) to dichotomies (*b*), or from dichotomies to trichotomies (*c*), or from trichotomies to little series (*d*).

The interpretation which seems to be called for is the following. First of all, a memory-image is not simply the prolongation of the perception of the model. On the contrary, it seems to act in a symbolic manner so as to reflect the subject's assimilation "schèmes",[2] that is, the way in which he *understood* the model (I say "understood", and not "copied", which is an entirely different thing). Now in six months, in the case of seriation or ordering, such as we have in this experiment, this operational or preoperational scheme of assimilation evolves, as the child has continued to compare objects of different sizes, etc., outside and well beyond the experiment which we presented to him.[3] Then the new scheme of the next level serves as the code for decoding the original memory. The final memory, then, is indeed a decoding, but it is the decoding of a code which has changed, which is better structured than it was before, and which gives rise to a new image which symbolizes the current state of the operational schema, and not what it was at the time when the encoding was done.

This first experiment gave rise to different variants, for example, having the subjects describe the model verbally at the time of encoding, instead of just having them look at it. This was done with the aim of getting at the possible role of language in the organization of the mnemonic code. In fact, there was very little difference, due to reasons which H. Sinclair has been able to clarify. This linguist-turned-psychologist has shown that language development (the proportion of "scalars" to "vectors" or of binary expressions to quaternary expressions, etc.) is dependent on operational development, and not the inverse. Sinclair's book on language and intellectual operations has just been published (Sinclair de Zwart, 1966)[4] and provides a collection of very new findings to this effect (notably on the relations between language and conservation, and the almost negligible effects of linguistic training on progress in conservation). This work constitutes the best experimental refutation of J. Bruner's hypothesis that language and symbolic functions constitute the principal factors in the formation of operational structures and conservation.

(B) The result of this first experiment seemed to us too good to be true, so we replicated it with another figure. This time it was an M-shaped series, with big sticks at each end, getting smaller towards the middle |ıı|. The memory was tested after one week and after 10 weeks. In this case the results are less spectacular, of course, because the model is more difficult (the second half of the figure being the inverse order of the first half). Nonetheless, after 10 weeks we found no regression, and 38% of the subjects (23 out of 61) made progress from one level to the next, once again without making leaps to the correct answer.

One other experiment which it may be useful to mention (from among about 20 which we have done) deals with the subject's operational system of spatial coordinates. We know from previous experiments that if children from 4 to 10 are shown a jar half full of water and asked to predict how the water will be if the bottle is tipped at various angles, it isn't until they are 9 or 10 years old that they can anticipate a horizontal level for all positions of the bottle. Until then, they predict the level to be curved, or to be tilted, parallel to the bottom or the side of the bottle, or cutting across a corner, but not horizontal. In this memory experiment, then, we showed the children a half-full bottle of water, tipped at 45°, and asked for recall an hour later, a week later, and six months later. In the first two cases, we find once again that the memory does not simply reproduce the original perception, but it represents the way the model was assimilated to the subject's operational structure: we found the very same levels that we had found in the earlier experiment when the subjects were asked to predict. But after six months, in 55 subjects we found 6 cases of regression (memories of a lower level than the memory after one week), 32 subjects who remained stationary (the same memory as before), and 17 who showed progress. Once again, the progress was generally from one level to the next. There was progress, then, in about 30% of the cases, but it is worthwhile noting that the percentage was highest among the children 7 to 9 years of age, that is, those who were closest to the right reaction, even though many children in this age group gave the right response from the outset, so their response did not change after six months. Finally, let us note some interesting cases where intellectual conflict was suppressed in memory: in some cases the bottle was presented to the child flat on its side, and some children remembered that the water was parallel to the side, but remembered the bottle in the more probable position of standing up, leading to the situation portrayed in Fig. 1a; in other cases, children represented the bottle as full of water, even though it had no cap (Fig. 1b).

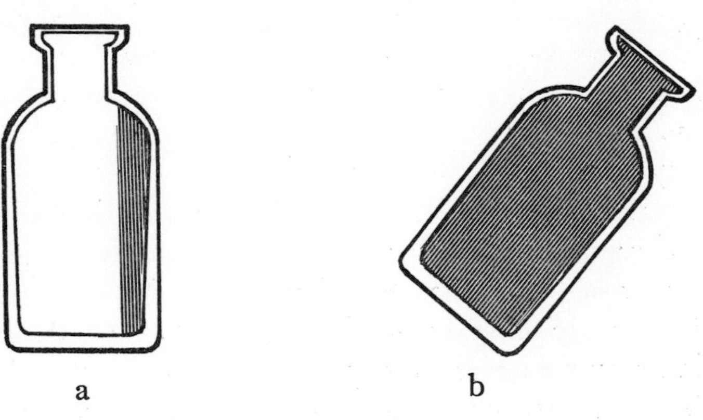

Figure 1

(C) But changes in the mnemonic code due to operational progress on the part of the subjects does not always lead to a better recollection six months later. We can present subjects with a model which gives rise to a conflict between two or more different and non-contemporary operational "schèmes". In these cases, the memory is still dominated by the operational "schèmes" which determine the code, but it shows certain deformations. These deformations are not haphazardous deteriorations; rather they are systematic, moving in the direction of a resolution of the conflict created by the operational schemata in question. One good example of such a situation is the following, which we studied with J. Bliss. We show the children 8 matches, arranged as shown in Fig. 2*a*. (The four matches arranged in the zig-zag pattern must be flattened out enough so that

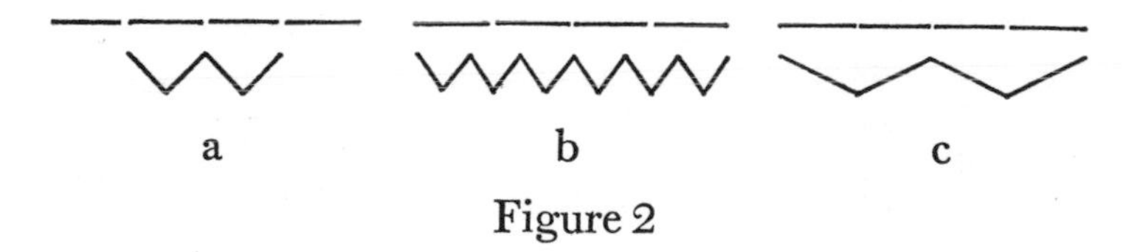

Figure 2

they are not seen as a W; if they are seen as a W the problem disappears.) Fig. 2*a* represents a conflict for young children: 1) there is numerical equivalence, since they see 4 matches and 4 matches, and they conclude that the lengths ought to be the same; 2) but since at that age their spatial notions are ordinal and not metric ("longer" means "goes farther"), they think that if the two lines of matches are the same length, they ought to have the same terminal points, which is not at all the case. There is a conflict between two operational or preoperational "schèmes", and the mnemonic code must then reveal systematic deformations tending towards the resolution of this conflict. This is exactly what our findings indicate, both after one week and after six months.

Most of the reproductions tend to make the two rows the same length, either (with the youngest children) by adding more matches (see Fig. 2*b*) or (with slightly older children) by conserving the same number, but making each match longer (Fig. 2*c*). Only relatively advanced subjects managed to remember the configuration as it was. We can see in these deformations (*b* and *c*) the influence of a sort of mnemonic inference, analogous to the unconscious perceptual inferences which Helmholtz hypothesized. After six months, this conflict between number and length results rather generally in a less adequate recollection; improvements are rather rare. Moreover, the correct representation, or errors which nonetheless conserve numerical equivalence (type *c*) are maintained after six months only by children of 7 years or older, that is, only at the level of the conservation of number. (Conservation of length is a slightly more complicated notion, acquired later than the conservation of number.)

The three types of memory

Another result of our research was to show the developmental difference among three types of memory: recognition, reconstruction, and evocation.[5]

The difference between recognition and evocation has been familiar for a long time. Recognition can rely on perception and sensori-motor "schèmes" alone, while evocation requires mental imagery or language, that is, some form of the symbolic function, some form of operational or preoperational representation. For this reason, there is no evocative memory in children before the age of 1½ or 2 years, while recognition memory is present during the first few months of life. Phylogenetically, recognition phenomena can be observed in lower invertebrates, while evocation seems to be specific to higher primates, or to man.

It is easy to demonstrate this difference in the experiments I have just described or in other similar ones. For example, in one experiment we presented two overlapping rings, with blue circles in the intersection, blue squares in one of the rings outside the intersection, and red circles in the other (Fig. 3). The evocation of this model six months later, by 5 to 8 year-olds, is rather poor, since the asymmetry of this intersection is not very natural at that age. (It is much less natural than a four-part matrix which includes red squares.) But if we present 10 choices, representing the reproductions of children in the evocation experiment (sepa-

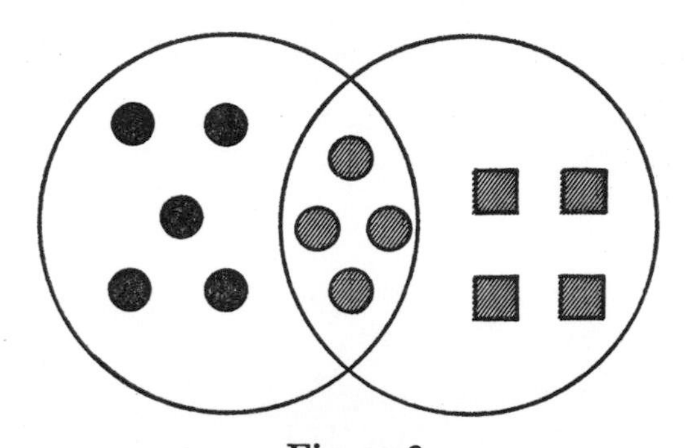

Figure 3

Cross-hatched = blue
Solid = green

rate circles, or collections without circles, etc.) and include the correct model, then 60% to 70% of the subjects recognize the correct one.

But between these two types of memory is an intemediate type which has not been given due attention, though it is certainly interesting for developmental psychology. This is reconstruction memory, which we can observe when we give the subject the material which was used to construct the model (along with some extra material), and ask him to rearrange the material in the configuration which he had seen earlier. This form of memory is similar to recognition, since the subject sees the elements of the model, without having to recall them; but there is also a form of evocation, since the elements must be arranged so as to replicate the original configuration, without the child's being able, at the time of reconstruction, to perceive the model as it was.

This form of memory has certainly been known for a long time, since Munsterberg, Ebbinghaus, and others used it as an experimental technique. But it is essential to emphasize its developmental importance, since it has a place between recognition memory and evocation memory. For instance, in a memory experiment dealing with matrices (four compartments containing red and blue squares and red and blue circles), when we compare the evocation results after 6 months with the results after 1 week, we find a regression in 61% of the subjects from 4 to 8 years. But when we look at the reconstruction results, we find regression among the 4 to 5 year-olds, but 48% progress among the 6 to 8 year olds.[6] The instructions simply asked them to reconstruct what they had "seen" six months earlier, without any reference to classification or matrices. Across the board, we found that reconstruction was always ahead of evocation, even in experiments where part of the figure was arbitrary. For example, in one of our experiments we presented two triangles, two squares, two circles, and two ellipses, but on each one was superimposed a bar, either long or short, and either horizontal or vertical. Both after one week and after six months, we found 50% better performance on reconstruction than on evocation. But in this case, we presented the model again after the last memory test, and then one week later (that is, 6 months and one week after the initial presentation), we studied their memory again. This time, there is a 75% better performance in reconstruction than in evocation.

Phylogenetically, too, we find that reconstructive memory comes between recognition and evocative memory. We can in fact think of imitation as a form of reconstructive memory, since this form of memory consists of imitating a model. We have said that recognition occurs in lower invertebrates, while evocation occurs only in man, or perhaps the higher primates. If we consider imitation to be a form of reconstruction, then this type of memory can be found in birds, and even in Von Frisch's bees.

Conclusion: memory and intelligence

Memory consists of two components. One of them is the figurative component, which is perceptual in the case of recognition, imitative in the case of reconstruction, and mental imagery in the case of the memory images necessary for evocation. The other is the operative component, which consists of action "schèmes," or representative "schèmes" (either preoperational or operational). The role of these "schèmes" has already been brought out by Bartlett in his *Remembering* and it is fundamental from the developmental point of view. It poses the question of the relationship between these "schèmes" and the figurative aspects of memory, particularly mental images.

Now the conservation of these "schèmes," which

in all of the preceding experiments seems to play an essential role in the memory mechanism, is in reality a problem of intelligence, more than of memory. A "schème" is that part of an action or operation which is repeatable and generalizeable in another action or operation; it is that part which is essentially characteristic of the action or operation. In this sense, the conservation of a "schème" depends directly on its own use, and is the result of its own functioning. Therefore, the memory of a "schème" is nothing other than the "schème" itself.

It is helpful, then, to distinguish what we might call "memory in a broad sense" and "memory in a strict sense." The former consists of the conservation of "schèmes," and it is essentially intelligence itself, to the extent that intelligence is used to reconstruct the past. The latter, which is brought into play in recognition, reconstruction, and evocation, is only the figurative aspect of the "schèmes," in particular (in the case of evocation), all the memory-images which are conserved only by being based on "schèmes." In fact everything that we have seen, in each of our experiments, shows the tight dependence of memory on the conservation and the development of "schèmes." This is what explains the progress of memory over six months, where the "schèmes" continue to develop, or the deterioration of memory where there is a conflict among two or more "schèmes," or where the "schèmes" are not adequate to support the memory-images.

In a word, memory seems to be a special case of

intelligent activity, applied to the reconstruction of the past rather than to knowledge of the present or anticipation of the future. In the case of what we call "logical memory," this statement is more or less obvious. As for rote memory, it seems to us that it simply never is encountered in an absolute form. Even what we might call rote memory is always schematized to one degree or another, and this schematization shows its relationship with the work of intelligence. It is true that there exist certain cases where memory seems to be disassociated from intelligence, as in certain famous cases of memory in the mentally abnormal, where memory seems to be a substitute for, and not an application of, intelligence. But even in these cases, memory seems to be a specialization of intellectual work; intelligence, surely deficient in these cases, specializes in reconstructing certain facts or events which would have no interest for a normal intelligence.[7]

If I am permitted one remark by way of conclusion, these few experiments have perhaps not taught us much about memory, but they have at least reassured us about the existence and the efficacy of operations. These operations, which we studied at first for their own sake, and mainly from the point of view of their logic, have subsequently shown themselves to be essential in the development of mental imagery (Piaget and Inhelder, 1966), of language (Sinclair de Zwart, 1966) and now of memory.

IDENTITY AND CONSERVATION[8]

FOR several years, we have been studying the development of the concept and perception of identity, and the relationship between the concept of identity and notions of conservation. I have recently learned that J. Bruner (1966) and other psychologists are looking into the same problem. This is an interesting convergence between bodies of research which are in fact independent; but it is a natural convergence, since it is normal to study identity sooner or later if we are concerned with conservation.

Introduction, definitions and statement of the problems

The obvious fact for all of us is that the concept of identity is much more precocious than conservation. But even to accept this statement we must agree on some definitions, because the concept of identity changes with development (as it does throughout the history of science and mathematics), and nothing remains less identical than the concept or the notion of identity.

We shall use the term "conservation" for notions which appear at about 7 or 8 years of age, and which affirm the existence of *quantitative* invariants. The conservation of substance, of weight, etc., thus deal with quantities of matter or weight. The conservation of a group, in the logical or mathematical sense, when the distribution of the parts or the sub-groups has been modified, deals with the "extension" of the group, that is, with the quantity of individual objects which make up the group. The conservation of number is surely quantitative, and so is that of weight, volume, etc.

But on the other hand, precisely because they are quantitative, notions of conservation always deal with invariants which are based on the *composition* of certain transformations, so that we can say that where there is no transformation we cannot speak of conservation.[9] For example, when we pour water from a wide glass to a narrow glass, the shape of the water is changed both in height and in width, and observation shows that either the subject only notices one (usually the height) or he notices both, but only as covariations, and not as compensations. Conservation is possible only when there is composition of quantitative variations, which can take the form of a compensation of relations (higher x thinner = the same amount), or simply of an additive composition (nothing added, nothing taken away = the same amount).

The essential characteristic of preoperational (that is, pre-conservational) identity, on the other hand, is that it deals with simple qualitative invariants, without any quantitative composition. For example, in the pouring of liquids, even a 4 or 5 year old, who maintains that the amount of water has changed, will admit that it is "the same water," in the sense that the nature of the matter "water" has not changed even if the quantity of that matter has changed. Similarly, if he draws his own body as he was when he was little and again as he is now, he will recognize that it is still the same individual, even if he is bigger in size ("It's still me"). In this case, the invariant is obtained without quantitative composition; there is simply a *dissociation* between a permanent quality (the same water, the same me) and the variable qualities (the shape or size), but there is no composition of these variations.

Thus defined, the first conservations appear around the age of 6½ or 7 years, and others continue to appear at 9-10 years, or as late as 11-12 years, because they are tied to the elaboration of quantitative notions which are very complex, and which require a transition from purely ordinal judgments (for instance, longer = goes farther) to extensive, numerical, or metric judgments. On the other hand, there are very early examples of qualitative identity, as early as the end of the sensori-motor period, because it does not necessitate quantification.

One might say that there is one notable exception to what I have just said, namely, the appearance between 9 and 12 months of the "schème" of the permanent object, which I myself have often considered to be the first form of conservation. In fact, that is a misuse of language; if we wish to conform to the preceding definitions, then the "schème" of the permanent object is a case of identity, and not of quantitative conservation. It is the identity of an object which does not vary quantitatively but remains the same while changing its position, or being hidden behind a screen.

Given these definitions, identity raises three general problems, each of which we shall treat briefly: (1) What is the nature of the notion of identity, compared with the nature of reversible operations? (2) What are the stages in its development, and the reasons for its early appearance? (3) How is it related to conservation? As far as the third question is concerned, the most interesting one to our way of thinking, identity can be seen, as J. Bruner sees it, as one of the stages in the formation of conservations, with direct continuity between them; or it can be seen, as we shall try to show, not as the source of conservations, but as one of its conditions. According to this second alternative, the roots of conservation would be found in the system of reversible operations, which alone permit quantification (or the coherent elaboration of various types of quantities). In this case, we could understand that identity is more precocious than conservations, and we could understand that later identity would be integrated into the systems of conservations, as one operation among many, while the conservations would depend on the whole system, and not only on identity.

The nature of identity

If we agree to call "operations" any actions which have been interiorized, which are reversible (addition and subtraction, for example), and which are coordinated into systems ("groupings," groups, lattices, etc.), then we can admit that identity can become at some point an operation among others, but only relatively late, at a rather advanced level, and as a part of a system of operations. For example, in an additive classification, where $A + A^1 = B$; $B + B^1 = C$, etc., we do have $A{=}A$, $B{=}B$, etc., but only on condition that $A - A = 0$ and $A + 0 = A$. The identity, $A = A$ depends on a regulator, the "identical operation" of a grouping, that is ± 0; from this point of view, identity has become operational only because it has been integrated into a system of operations.

But this is a late development (7 or 8 years) and there exist preoperational identities long before these systems of operations have been established. Preoperational qualitative identities can very well exist in situations where there is no sign of any of the fundamental rules of operations, such as reversibility and transitivity.

For example, in one experiment which we carried out with G. Voyat, 3 to 5 year-olds who took apart a necklace and spread out the beads in a box, said that the beads were "still the same necklace," calling on a notion of identity by assimilation to their own action; but if they started from the separate beads, without having made the necklace, they naturally did not say that the beads were the same as the necklace: identity here thus depends on the chronological order of the actions, and is not reversible. Similarly (in another experiment with Voyat to which we shall return), if the children draw several steps in the growth of a plant, calling them A, B, C, etc., they will admit the identity of A with B, B with C, C with D, but before 7 years of age they will not admit the identity of A with D (saying, "it's not the same plant any more"); here, the identity is not transitive.

However, well before it becomes operational, identity is already a logical instrument. I have often maintained that preoperational structures were prelogical, but drawing attention all the while to what I have called "articulated intuitions," that is, partial coordinations which sketch out future operations. Now we have found that there is indeed a sort of preoperational logic, much broader than the notion of identity, which makes up in a way the first half of operational logic, that is, an oriented system which is sufficient as long as it is oriented in the right direction, but which lacks the inverse orientation, or in other words, reversibility. This preoperational logic is the logic of functions, that is, of ordered couples, one-way "applications," etc., and it leads to the discovery of co-properties, of co-variations, and other *functional relationships* of the form $y = f(x)$.

Now preoperational identity is one aspect of these elementary functions. Let us take as an example a string, pulled down by a weight at end b. The child discovers

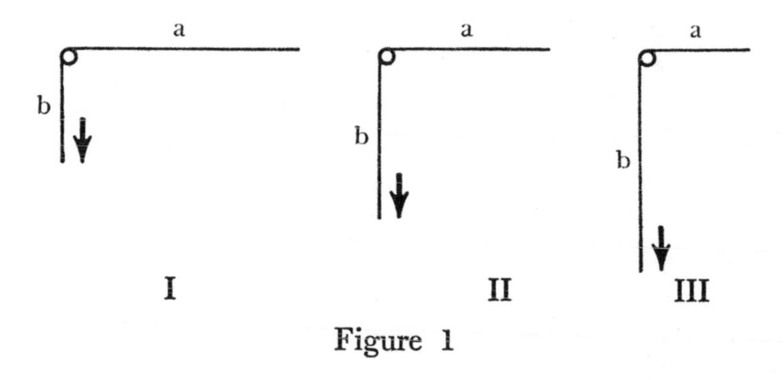

Figure 1

easily the co-variation involved: if the segment a becomes shorter, then the segment b becomes longer. He discovers just as easily the co-property, which is even an identity: "it's the same string," which gets shorter in the segment a and longer in the segment b. And, significantly, he discovers this well before arriving at the conservation of length $a+b$. This conservation, no matter how long the segment b or a may be, is reached at about 7 or 8 years of age, while the co-variation and identity are affirmed at 4 or 5 years of age. Here, then, is an example of the absence of operational quantification and conservation, since the quantities remain ordinal: "longer" and "shorter" are still judged in terms of "farther" and "not as far," based simply on the endpoints, but that in no way precludes the use of functions or qualitative identity.

We might say, then, that this logic of functions and of qualitative identity is just half of the logic of reversible operations, because it is based on directed actions, or, in other words, the concept of order, which appears so fundamental, and which plays such an important role (sometimes correctly, sometimes with error) in preoperational intuitions where topological and ordinal notions of boundaries remain so long predominant. In general terms, we can say that the essential instrument of this semi-logic is that of *correspondence,* but of one-way correspondence which lacks the reciprocity which alone guarantees equivalences and conservations. For example, a 5 or 6 year old will use *"applications"* of the type "many-to-one," which are already truly functions, in the mathematical sense, but usually they will lack the inverse correspondence, "one-to-many," which is no longer a simple "application," and which is necessary for the construction of equivalence classes and their inclusions. Even in the case of one-to-one correspondence they often lack reciprocity. A Belgian mathematician did the following experiment at our center in Geneva. A little truck takes a random route through a collection of houses, A, B, C, etc., picking up a colored token in front of each house (there is a different color for each house, while a little man of the same color stays in front of the house, to establish a color-house correspondence). These tokens are placed in the truck in the order in which they are picked up, and at the end of the trip the child is asked why the tokens are in that order. From the age of 5, children are easily able to show that the tokens correspond to the order in which they were picked up in front of the houses. But if we then ask them to retrace the truck's route, it is only at 7 or 8 years of age that they are able to reconstitute the sequence of stops in front of the houses, as if the reciprocal correspondence were more difficult than the direct correspondence. (For the details of this experiment, see Van den Bogaerts-Rombouts, 1966.)

In a word, preoperational identity is one aspect of a partial logic, the logic of functions which translates the sense of direction of actions themselves; but this logic lacks the general reversibility which would be necessary for the elaboration of quantities and the instruments of quantification.

Precocity and development of the notion of identity

First of all, let us recall that identity evolves during development; it evolves a good deal, in fact. Nothing remains identical during normal mental evolution, not even identity, in spite of its very function; and this is precisely because it changes its function from one stage to another. There are a certain number of experiments which we have done, with G. Voyatt and M. Bovet in the area of concepts, and with Vinh-Bang and Droz in the area of perception. We shall deal only with concepts here.

One of these experiments consists of presenting the child with a wire which can be made into an arc, or a straight line, and asking in each case if it is the same piece of wire, the same object, etc. We find four successive levels, which no doubt correspond to stages of a sort. At the first level (3 or 4 years) the children do not question the identity and base it essentially on the assimilation of the object to their possible actions: we can make an arc with a straight line or vice versa, so it is still the same object, with which we can do many things.[10] At the second level (4-5 years), the child starts to take an interest in the object itself, as well as in the action which can modify it; or more precisely, to take an interest in the objective modifications themselves, as well as in the ability to produce them. So he often concludes (although this second level may not be very general) that the object is no longer the same object because it changed its form. At the third level, the subject makes still more progress toward objective analysis, and begins to dissociate the permanent qualities from the variable qualities. It is, then, "the same object" since it is still the same piece of wire, but it has changed shape. But this qualitative identity does not yet imply conservation.

The child thinks that in changing its form, the wire changes its length; the straight line is longer than the arc since it goes beyond it. He still lacks metric quantifications, for judging intervals, and he still bases his idea of length on an ordinal judgment comparing the end-points. Finally, at the fourth level, the child attains the conservation of length as well as the identity of the object. But the conservation is not directly derived from the identity. It requires a new composition, based on the intervals between the end-points, and thus on a system of additive inclusions, within which identity is integrated, without constituting the source.

Similarly, with G. Voyat, we studied the identity of water as it was poured from one glass to another, or of a piece of modeling clay as it was given different shapes. Is it "the same water," "the same clay," etc.? The stages are the same, except that the second is often shortened, according to the type or the magnitude of the differences.

But now let us look at the analysis of an irreversible process, that is, a process which takes place in time, without any possibility for operational reversibility or even for a physical, empirical return to the point of departure. Growth is such a process.

Voyat began with the growth of a bean, but it was too slow! Then he used a solution of copper sulphate in water, in which he "planted" a grain of potassium ferrocyanide; in a few minutes this gives an arborescent growth something like a seaweed. The child watches this phenomenon, and then we ask him to make some drawings of steps in the growth of this "seaweed," and we have him order them. Then we ask whether his drawings, A, B, C, . . . N, represent "the same seaweed" (or "the same plant," etc., according to the term he uses). Then we ask him to draw himself during his own growth, when he was a little baby, a little bigger, etc., and we question him about the identity of his own body, or of himself. Finally, we have him do the same with the experimenter. In the cases where the subject did not assert the identity of the seaweed during its growth, we come back again to this question to see whether the identity of the child's own body during its growth brings out the identity of the seaweed.

We find at least three levels in the children's responses. In the first one, the child accepts easily the identity of his own body, in spite of the differences in size ("It's still me"), and the identity of the experimenter is accepted also. But in the case of the plant, he accepts certain identities (A = B or G = H), but he refuses to accept the identity if the difference is too great (A to H, for instance): "it grew, but it isn't the same any more; here it's a little plant and there it's a big plant, it's not the same plant." Once they have accepted the identity of their own body, and we return to the question of the "seaweed," they continue to deny this latter identity. At a second level, the initial reactions are the same, but when we come back to the question of the "seaweed," the child modifies his position, and accepts the identity of the plant. Finally, after about 7 or 8 years of age, the three types of identity are accepted without any problem.

This experiment is instructive in that it shows us at one and the same time both the difficulties presented by the notion of identity during growth, and the precocity of this notion in the case of the child's own body. At first glance, the origins of identity would seem to be bi-polar, if we go back as far as the sensori-motor level: the permanent object on the one hand and one's own body on the other. But we must bear in mind that one's own body is discovered and known only in relation to other human bodies, as J. M. Baldwin has emphasized in his essays on the role of imitation. In addition, Th. Gouin-Decarie has demonstrated the synchronization and the correlation between the discovery of object permanency (as we have outlined it) and the establishment of objectal relations (in the Freudian sense) which includes a more and more systematic interest in other human bodies (cf. Gouin-Decarie, 1966a). Finally, as I had hypothesized on the basis of observation, and as Gouin-Decarie (1966b) has verified experimentally, the first object to become permanent is another human body. It would seem, then, that the roots of identity are to be found in the complex involving "own body x body of another x permanent object." This complex is not bipolar, but derives from the functional unity of the exchanges between the subject and his physical and interpersonal surroundings, and is reinforced by the interplay of all the subject's objectivized actions, and particularly his instrumental actions.

In light of this, G. Voyat questioned subjects on the identity of the movement itself in an instrumental action: the subject, A, throws a ball, B, to hit another ball, C, and the question is whether it is the "same movement" which is transmitted from A to C; in another situation, the subject, A, is replaced by a release mechanism A^1. We found three levels of reaction. At the first level, the identity is affirmed in both cases, because of assimilation to action. At the second level, the subject takes an interest in the objective conditions of the movement (loss of speed, etc.) and reacts differently to the two conditions: when he himself throws the ball, he says it is "just one throw," it is "my throw" which is transmitted to C; but if the mechanism throws it, he does not see it as the same movement through B to C. There is a clear analogy between these results and the results of the plant and the child's own body.

Identity and Conservation

The facts presented so far show how much the notion of identity evolves during a child's development. It appears early as a preoperational notion, and even a sensori-motor schema, as a qualitative identity and as a projection of relations between the child's body and other objects, as he acts upon them. Later, it takes the form of an "identical operation," integrated into operational structures which make possible quantification and conservation.

In a recent book which he was so kind as to dedicate to me, Bruner (1966) hypothesizes that conservations are simply identities, generalized through language, etc. He thinks that conservation does not result from reversibility since, according to him, one can find cases of reversibility without conservation. Similarly, conservation does not result from compensation, since once again he claims that there are cases of compensation without conservation. Conservation, then, would simply be a generalization of the notion of identity, due to development of the symbolic instruments of thought.

Before approaching the heart of this discussion, which is the central problem of our lecture today, I should like to note that the dialogue with Bruner is rather difficult, since there are certain elementary distinctions which he does not make and, from my point of view, the absence of these distinctions necessarily gives rise to a certain confusion. I should like to mention three of these distinctions:

(1) First, we must distinguish *co-variations* (which are functional) from compensations (which are operational). For example, when we asked 5-to 6-year olds to predict where the water level would be in a thin glass when the water was poured from a wider glass, 23% anticipated that the water would rise higher in the thin glass, but once it was done, they denied the conservation (cf. Piaget and Inhelder, 1966, p. 310). Bruner

would say that this is a case of compensation without conservation, but in fact it is not compensation: it is simply the prediction of a co-variation, due to previous experience (a child may have noticed this co-variation already when he has seen liquids poured, but this is a simple function, and not an operation); the subject does not understand that what is gained in height is lost in width, which alone constitutes compensation and leads to conservation.

(2) Secondly, we must distinguish true conservation from pseudo-conservation, which is easy enough with certain control experiments. For example, in the liquid-pouring experiment done behind a screen, which we ourselves did some time ago (Piaget and Inhelder, 1966, Chap. VIII), we often find 5-year-olds who say that there will be "as much to drink" in the thin glass as in the wide glass (it is even the general rule, with the exception of the 23% mentioned above). But this is a pseudo-conservation, because they also predict that the water level will stay the same in the thinner glass. The control experiment then is to present the child with two empty glasses, one wide and one thin, and ask him to pour the same amount into each glass (so that it's fair, etc.). Pseudo-conservation subjects pour the water *to the same level* in each glass, without seeing that one contains much more than the other (this is an example of ordinal evaluation, based on the end-point, without any metric evaluation). Bruner did not do this control

experiment, so that many of the "conservations" he cites are simply pseudo-conservations.

(3) In the third place, Bruner does not distinguish reversibility, which is a logical and operational notion, from an empirical return, which is a physical notion (we have referred to it for many years as "an empirical return to the point of departure"). I am not convinced by his examples of reversibility without conservation: they are simply cases of empirical return, as an elastic band comes back to its original size if it is stretched and released.

(4) I should like to make one more point before continuing. Bruner constantly attributes to language a role which has in no way been verified. As we saw briefly in the lecture on memory (the preceding lecture) the work of Sinclair de Zwart (1966) gives clear evidence to the effect that a child's language is subordinated to his operational level, and does not constitute the formative mechanism of the operations.

Now let us come back to the problem of the relations between identity and conservation. Our hypothesis is that conservation is not simply a generalization of identity, and we base this hypothesis on the two following reasons. First, the identity of an object is derived simply by *dissociating the permanent qualities* from its variable qualities – and that is why it appears so early. Second, conservation necessitates a composition of quantitative transformations, according to the rules of operational composition – which is why it appears so late. (Note that I said the rules of operational composition, and not linguistic composition, for reasons which I mentioned above.)

The whole question, then, becomes that of establishing whether *quantities* are disccovered in the same way as *qualities,* or if they necessitate a real construction, that is, a more complex process of elaboration. Now it is clear that qualities can be identified simply through perception: color, shape, etc., are apprehended without any particular construction, and without going beyond the laws of perception. But the only quantitative relations apprehended by this means at the preoperational levels are ordinal and local evaluations. So expressions like "darker," "bigger," "wider," "heavier," etc., are at first understood only as comparisons which imply a partial, one-way order, and not a complete seriation with ordered ranks and inclusions which can run in either direction.[11] For example, "longer" is understood in the sense of "going farther," with the arrival point being a privileged center of attention, and the departure point or the interval between the two being neglected.

Quantity in the true sense requires much more, whether it be numerical or metric, or even relative to the extension of classes ($A < B$ if $B = A + A^1$) or to the inclusion of order positions ("distance" A – B is smaller than "distance" A – C if B falls between A and C). Quantity is necessarily based on a system of inclusions, which takes into account the intervals, or the complementary classes. Now such an inclusion is not a perceptual given, but must be constructed operationally, which is why quantitative conservations are so late appearing. If language alone imposed these structures, as J. Bruner believes, then of course the evolution would be much faster, since there would be no need for the child to build the structures himself, and he would receive ready-made, through linguistic training, all the instruments he needed. Unfortunately, the facts reveal the opposite situation, and we all know that, even at our age, we succeed in talking well only if we begin thinking well. But thinking means structuring reality by means of operations. I know that Bruner does not believe, or declares that he does not believe, in operations, but this is true only in appearance, since he locates them implicitly in language, and above all since he uses "identity" or identification as if it were a real operation, even according it much more power than it actually has.

Quantification is then the product of operational structures of increasing complexity, spreading over classification (with inclusion of extensions), and seriation as well as numerical "groups" and spatial measurement. Identity does not disappear with the onset of operations, but it is integrated into structures which go far beyond it, and which encompass it as one operation among many. This process is clearly visible in the very arguments which a 7 or 8 year old uses to justify the conservations which these structures make possible.

In fact, in all forms of conservation, these arguments come down to three, one of which is identity, which has become operational, and is tightly linked to the two others. The first of these arguments is reversibility by inversion: you have changed A to B, but you could change it back again from B to A and you would have the same A again. The second argument is reversibility through reciprocity or compensation: in changing A to B, you changed aspect x of A to x^1, greater than x, and aspect y of A to y^1, less than y, so that the two compensate each other, $x^1 y^1 = xy$. The third argument seems to be a simple identity: you didn't add anything or take anything away, so it's still the same amount. But in fact this identity raises a curious problem. The young subjects who deny conservation also know very well that nothing has been added or taken away, but this knowledge does not lead them to conservation. So it is not identity as such which is new in the reasoning of the 7-8 year olds; what is new is that now it has become an argument in favor of conservation whereas until that point it in no way implied conservation. What has happened to give identity this power which it did not have before? The point is that this is no longer the same identity. The qualitative identity "it's the same water" does not lead to the same thing at all. But the notion of "nothing added" is the quantitative and operational identity "+0," and the notion of "nothing taken away" is the quantitative and operational identity "—0". The composition "+0—0=0" is the "identity operation" of an operational grouping, and this operation can only take form in conjunction with the other operations, and as a part of their total system (the additive system, etc.). It is in this sense that we believe that the structure of a "grouping" of operations as such has a profound psychological meaning, and not only a logical one.

It is, then, the total system or grouping which is responsible for the formation of the conservations, and not identity. Identity is but one element of the system, and an element which has been transformed by the system itself, rather than being the source of the system.

FOOTNOTES

Memory and Operations of Intelligence

1. This lecture is based on a book to be published under the title "Mémoire et Intelligence", (J. Piaget and B. Inhelder, in collaboration with H. Sinclair) by Presses Universitaires de France, Paris 1968.

2. *Editor's Note*: Piaget distinguishes (in French) between "schema" and "schème", the former referring to an iconic representation, while the latter has no figural connotation. Since Piaget intends the non-figurative meaning here, the French term is retained.

3. Let us note in passing that the development is not purely endogenic, as I am often understood – wrongly – to be saying. It requires interactions between maturation, practice, and experiences – thus, the subject's total action.

4. References are listed in alphabetical order at the end of the second lecture.

5. *Editor's note*: Piaget's distinction between "recognition" and "evocation" appears to parallel closely that which is usually made between recognition and *reproduction* (or between recognition and recall, with respect to verbal memory).

But since the latter distinction is defined rather in methodological terms, while the term "evocation" as used by Piaget has more of a process connotation, it seemed best to retain the literal translation of this term.

6. Once again, this progress is small in any given subject; we do not find sudden leaps to the correct matrix form, which might be explained simply by an operational construction at the time of the test, without any memory activity.

7. Dr. Simon, Binet's collaborator, once showed me in a mental clinic near Paris, a mentally deficient child with a chronological age of 24 years and a mental age of 7 years (according to Binet-Simon tests). He had learned by heart the days of the week of 13 centuries; when asked what day of the week was July 7, 1409, he replied immediately (not a single error in ½ hour of questions). Here, then, is an excellent example of specialization of a modest intelligence on a problem which is of no interest to us.

Identity and Conservation

8. This lecture is based on a volume of "Études d'épistémologie génétique", Presses Universitaires de France, Paris 1968.

9. Conversely, one could say that it is because conservations are always based on a composition of transformations that they are always quantitative. Even in the conservation of order (for example, where ABC, permuted to CBA conserves the relation of "between," since B is between A and C as well as between C and A) there is a quantitative relation since when we say that B is between A and C, we are saying that the interval AB is smaller than interval AC.

10. Let us note that identity is facilitated here by the fact that the action can be undone empirically. But this empirical re-

turn must not be confused with reversibility. When actions are cancelled empirically, the two actions are distinct – e.g., bending and straightening. A reversible operation, on the other hand, is one and the same operation, taking place either in one direction or in the other, like uniting and separating, for instance.

11. Moreover, Sinclair de Zwart (1966) has shown that although pre-conservational children understand expressions such as "A is *smaller* than B" (vectors, as these expressions are called by linguists) they *use* only what linguists call scalars such as "A is *small* and B is *big*," etc. This is also to be found in the early levels of seriation.

BIBLIOGRAPHY

Bruner, J. S. (ed.) *Studies in cognitive growth*. New York: Wiley, 1966.

Gouin-Decarie, T. *Intelligence and affectivity in early childhood*. New York: International Universities Press, 1966. (a)

Gouin-Decarie, T. Intelligence sensori-motrice et psychologie du premier age. In *Psychologie et épistémologie génétiques: Thèmes Piagétiens*. Paris: Dunod, 1966. Pp. 299-306. (b)

Piaget, J., and Inhelder, B. *L'image mentale chez l'enfant*. Paris: Presses Universitaires de France, 1966.

Sinclair de Zwart, H. *Acquisition du langage et développement de la pensée*. Paris: Dunod, 1966.

Van den Bogaert-Rombouts, N. Projection spatiale d'une série temporelle. In Grize, J.B., al., *L'Épistemologie du temps*. Paris: Presses Universitaires de France, 1966. Pp. 137-148. (Études d'Épistemologie génétique, XX)